W9-BHO-594

B. TRAVEN
The Creation of the Sun and the Moon

illustrated by Alberto Beltrán

LAWRENCE HILL & CO.
CREATIVE ARTS BOOK CO.
Westport • Berkeley
1977

Published by
Lawrence Hill & Co., 24 Burr Farms Road, Westport, Conn. 06880
and Creative Arts Book Co., 833 Bancroft Way, Berkeley, Calif. 94710

The Creation of the Sun and the Moon

There is a legend among the Indians of Mexico that tells how once when the world was young the Sun brought joy to men, how the Sun was destroyed by evil, and how a singularly brave young Indian undertook a perilous journey to create a new Sun.

And this is how the legend goes.

The Creation of the Sun and the Moon

Once men lived in peace on earth and in true happiness. The golden Sun gave them light and warmth, enriched their fields with corn, painted the flowers in radiant colors, filled the trees with sweet fruit in abundance, and caused the birds to sing.

Thus it was only natural for men to revere the Sun as the source of all blessings and richness and happiness on earth. To thank the good gods for the Sun, men built great temples and pyramids of stone and sang beautiful songs of praise.

But the gods of evil and darkness envied the happiness that men enjoyed on earth. So it came to pass that these gods left the deep ravines where they lived and their homes on the shores of subterranean lakes and rivers and went forth to do

battle with the good gods so that they might destroy them and rule the world.

The fierce fight between the gods of good and evil shook the universe to its foundations. The seas and lakes and rivers rose up, flooding fields and houses and whole cities.

After the floods receded, a terrible drought came and with it misery over all the lands. It was only the Sun, still bright in the sky, that gave hope to the people and kept alive their faith that the good gods would conquer.

The long and bitter battle raged but in the end the gods of evil triumphed. They had united with the enemies of all that was good—with the evil spirits of intolerance and brutality, greed and envy, vanity and meanness and jealousy—and so grew powerful enough at last to win a complete victory. In their meanness they slew all their adversaries and left the bodies of the good gods unburied for the zopilotes and vultures and coyotes to devour.

There was sadness and mourning everywhere

in the universe; no longer was there peace and harmony. Instead of harmony and good will only discord and enmity arose whenever people came together.

The good gods had been destroyed, but men still worshiped the Sun. The gods of evil were ill with envy and they set out to destroy the Sun once and for all.

They hated the Sun because of its light and warmth and friendliness to the people on earth. They wished to extinguish the Sun in the hope of annihilating all mankind. For mankind had been the creation of the good gods, and the first people on earth were as children of the first gods, with the laughing goodness and the warm breath of the gods themselves.

So now the triumphant gods of evil, commanding mountains of ice and snow and freezing storms, extinguished the Sun, and darkness settled over all the earth.

All plants and trees and all grasses were now covered with snow and ice. Only some wild maize still grew, and in a few places protected by wooded hills some stalks of beans and edible roots survived.

No longer did trees bear fruit or adorn the earth with blossoms. Even strong old trees withered away, and the birds, with no possibility to nest, forgot how to sing. The crickets and cicadas in the fields grew silent, too, and the beetles and bees ceased to hum in the woods and bushes. No more did butterflies—the crown jewels of the good gods —brighten the air. And the earth's dome, once the playground of fantastically formed multicolored birds, was now empty, gray, and silent.

People died of starvation. Many died from the cold. And many others lost their way in the unending darkness, never to find their homes again. They could no longer count the days and so lost all sense of time. All over the world people knew hunger and death and suffering.

Then at last, when desperation was at its highest, the kings and lords and leaders of all the Indian peoples called a great gathering to discuss

the creation of a new Sun, whose light would conquer the gods of darkness.

The only light left in the universe was the faint light of the stars high up in the sky. The gods of evil had wished to leave mankind in utter darkness, but they had not been able to put out the stars. On the stars there existed the spirits of departed humans and to them the good gods had given the strength and wisdom to keep the stars shining forever. The stars were the very substance

of the universe, and only from their light, the sages in the temples declared, could a new Sun be created.

The meeting of the kings and chieftains lasted for seven long weeks, and in all that time not one man could tell another how to make a new Sun. At last one among them remembered that in the temple of the Tigermen and Snakegods, that is, in Tonaljá—the source of the waters high above valleys and plains—there lived an ancient philosopher. He was more than three hundred years old. His name was Bayelsnael, and it was said that all the secrets of nature were known to him.

Bayelsnael was summoned to the council and to him was put the question: How could a new Sun be created so that mankind might survive?

After a time of meditation, Bayelsnael spoke to the council and he said: "Hear ye, esteemed kings and princes and chieftains, mighty lords, brothers, and friends! There is a way to create a new Sun as big and beautiful as the Sun we once enjoyed. But the way is difficult and full of danger. A young and strong man of Indian blood must visit the stars. He must ask the spirits that dwell there to give him a small piece of each star. Though star-fragments are hotter than any fire known on earth, yet he must be able to hold them in his hands. For he must fasten each star-piece onto his shield, and he must then climb higher and higher, gathering fragments from the stars, until he reaches the very apex in the arc of the sky. There, when all the star-pieces are fastened at last on his shield, the shield

itself will turn into a great flaming sun."

After Bayelsnael had spoken, all the kings and chieftains and bravest warriors leaped up and cried out in a mighty voice: "We are ready to go and create a new Sun!"

The old man answered them calmly.

"It speaks well that all are so ready to go. But only one man may do so, and this one must go alone with his great shield, because only one Sun is to be created. More than one Sun would burn the earth to ashes.

"And I must tell you that the brave man who is willing to go must be prepared for the greatest sacrifice a man can make. He must leave his wife and children, his father and mother, his friends and his people. Never again can he return to earth. He must wander forever in the sky, shield in one hand, lance in the other, always ready to fight the evil gods. For the gods of darkness will not rest. Again and again they will try to put out the light of the Sun, which is their enemy.

"Thus he who aspires to create a new Sun may look down upon the earth for ever and ever, but he can never return to it. He will see his loved ones, his friends, and all his people die, one after another, but he himself will be immortal—for all eternity. The older he grows, the more strange his people will become to him. He will be a lonely soul in the universe—lonely forever. Think carefully of this, each one of you, before you decide to try."

When the kings and lords and warriors, and all

men had heard these words of warning, they lost heart and fell silent. Who among them would wish to separate himself, forever, from his wife and his children, his father and mother and friends? Here on earth they could die peacefully among their loved ones. All feared to live forever—never to die. Here on earth they could see how men were born, how they flourished, how they withered into old age and died peacefully at last; but the hero in the skies bearing aloft his burning shield would never be able to share the destinies of men on earth. Nor would he be able to hope, to suffer, to rejoice, and thus live life in its full sense among other men. And should he look down from the sky and see misery and disaster coming upon mankind, he would be unable to help or even to warn his own people.

All this was more than the bravest of the warriors dared to undertake. They had experienced much, and they knew well that they lacked the strength and courage to leave their people and to endure all that had been described to them as the destiny of the one who would create a new Sun.

A deep silence settled over the council—a silence that lasted for seven long days. Then on the morning of the eighth day, one of the younger of the chieftains raised his voice and said:

"With your permission, noble lords and warriors, allow me to speak. I am young, strong, and experienced in the use of arms. My wife is young and beautiful; I love her dearly, for she is the very image of kindness and goodness. I have a fine son, noble of mind and strong in body, versatile as a young tiger, shrewd as a coyote, swift as an antelope. I have a mother who is now old and weak, to who I am protector and all her hope. I can also count twelve if not more good friends whose faithfulness I have valued since childhood days, because with them I shared dangers and hunger, wounds and thirst. I am a true son of this earth, neither better nor worse than any of my people; yes, I am in fact part of the earth, as my breath is part of the air beneath the sky.

"Yet, what use is all of this to me when my

people are without a Sun? How can I be happy here on earth when, more and more, all men are suffering! Without a Sun, men will perish and disappear from the earth. For that reason, noble kings and chieftains, I ask submissively your permission to leave earth and go forth to create a new Sun; though I am the youngest among you, wise men of all tribes and kingdoms, I pray you, give me your permission to do my duty to you and to mankind.

"Kings and chieftains, do not think that I desire to rise above the members of this great council, nor do I seek glory and honor for great deeds. Every man in this council is more worthy than I. But in these seven long days of silence, I have come to understand that every king, chieftain, and honorable man in this council has a larger duty to his family, his friends, his people, and to earth than have I, the youngest and least experienced among you. Thus, coming to the end of my words, it is I who must go to create a new Sun, be my fate and destiny what they will be."

He who spoke thus, in the longest speech of his life, was Chicovaneg, a young chieftain of the Shcucchuistans, a tribe of the Tzeltal nation of Indians living in southern Mexico.

The lords and the warriors of the council

listened and for a time they were silent. Each felt in the heaviness of his heart all that lay before this youngest one among them should they grant his request. Yet each knew too that a new Sun must be kindled if men were to survive. So at last they gave their consent.

Chicovaneg took leave of his wife and his son, of his mother, his friends, and his people. And none spoke of what was most in his thoughts, that this was indeed a last farewell.

Then Chicovaneg went to seek the counsel of the old sage of Tonaljá. Bayelsnael told him in what manner he must equip himself for his great quest, and this the young chieftain went forth to do.

First he made himself a strong shield. He made it from the hides of kingly tigers, and wove among the hides the skin of a mighty coatl tapir, which he caught near the lake of Pelhaj in the very depths of the jungle. Then he made himself a living helmet out of a powerful eagle which lived on the highest mountain peaks overlooking the plains of Quentan.

Then he went forth to look for the Feathered Serpent.

The Feathered Serpent was the living symbol of the universe, of all friendly things that flew in the air or moved on earth and in its waters. The gods of darkness abhorred this symbol of goodness. Although they had seized and overcome the Feathered Serpent, they were powerless to destroy it, for it was life itself.

Chicovaneg sought the Feathered Serpent in vain through many perilous encounters. Then at last he had the help of a Quetzal.

This Quetzal was considered a noble being among the trogons. He was the most glorious of all multicolored birds and was revered by man and beast alike. But this day, hunted for his beautiful plumage, he had been wounded and had fallen into a lake; and Chicovaneg, searching the shore for traces of the Feathered Serpent, saw the bird struggling in the water. He took off his heavy clothes and swam out to save the Quetzal.

An evil spirit hidden in the high rushes of the lake observed all this. Seizing a fish as swift and ferocious as a small shark, he sent it to inform the evil spirits at the bottom of the lake that the one who planned to create a new Sun was at this very moment swimming in the lake without protection.

Immediately a violent tempest came upon the lake. Heavy foaming waves arose, and rushing whirlpools gripped Chicovaneg, sucking him toward their depths. But with strong strokes he swam onward until he reached the Quetzal bird.

He placed the Quetzal on his head and the bird guided him back to shore, for the sharp eyes of the Quetzal were able to discern every distant threatening wave and every treacherous current. Then Chicovaneg made camp on the shore and nursed the wounded bird until his wing was healed.

When the Quetzal was again able to fly, he said to Chicovaneg: "I will guide you to the Feathered Serpent."

Thus Chicovaneg learned that the Feathered Serpent was tied in a cavern near a place called Tulhlum, where the sorcerer Masqueshab lived. Masqueshab was a most evil sorcerer, with four heads, forty eyes, eight arms, and eight legs, and he had earned his name from his great wickedness. The gods of darkness gave him much gold and many fine pearls which they had stolen from the temples of Tonaljá and Chamo, from Socton and Sotslum and Shimoljol, from Huniquibal and other sacred cities in the land.

Masqueshab had tied the Feathered Serpent to a rock in the depths of the cavern. He engaged a wicked man, called Molevaneg, as guard. Molevaneg had a crippled foot which kept him permanently in an evil temper so that he enjoyed torturing and tormenting the Feathered Serpent. The Serpent's cries of pain were a delight to Molevaneg. But one night the Feathered Serpent sank

his fangs into Molevaneg's crippled foot and held him fast, day and night, until Molevaneg withered and died. Then the Serpent released him and let him fall.

The death cries of Molevaneg were heard by the sorcerer Masqueshab. He hurried to the cavern, but found there no Molevaneg, only a heap of bone dust.

At this very time, Chicovaneg came along, disguised with beard and ugly warts and hunched-up back. Masqueshab asked him if he thought he could serve as a prisoner's guard. "I am a good guard of snakes," answered Chicovaneg. "I catch snakes for their skins, you see, and no snake escapes me, no matter how long, fast, or powerful."

So clever was Chicovaneg's disguise and so truly had he spoken in the accents of a common Indian woodman that the sorcerer did not recognize him. He made Chicovaneg the guard of the Feathered Serpent.

Now, cunningly, Chicovaneg planned to kill the evil sorcerer so that he could free the Serpent.

He made him drunk with a mixture of sweet juices of maguey, the aguamiel, and acorn, sugar-cane juice, and nance, and prickly pear and wild honey. With his four heads and forty eyes, eight arms and eight legs, Masqueshab, when he slept, was like a giant tarantula or octopus. Ten eyes were open while his other eyes slept. But Chicovaneg made him so drunk that he closed his forty eyes at once. Then Chicovaneg killed him with a spear poisoned with one hundred different venoms, given him by the old sage Bayelsnael.

Now Chicovaneg tried to free the Feathered Serpent from the rock. But the ropes were tied and knotted by tricks of darkest witchcraft. Chicovaneg then worked his own Indian magic learned from his own grandfathers. He sang sweet songs and melodies; and he danced in front of the cavern the dance of the hunter and the antelope, and the dance of the turtles, then the dance of the vivid Quetzal birds when in love, and then the dance of the tigers, and the dance of the hundred fires. And he danced the dance of the flowers in the night, and the dance of the butterflies at the Ushumacintla river; and at last, after many days, his magic rhythms freed the Feathered Serpent from the ropes and the rock. And the great sacred Serpent was glad for his freedom and strength. Recognizing in Chicovaneg the kindler of the new Sun, the grateful Serpent followed him from that day onward, obeying all his commands.

Chicovaneg set out on his great journey toward the stars. After many, many years and countless fights with evil spirits, he arrived at the ends of the world, as it was then. Here he found the lowest star so close that it seemed he could reach it with his hands.

He captured two powerful eagles, and because the eagles were of royal blood and were messengers of the good gods, he begged their forgiveness for having taken them.

But the eagles said: "We know well why you captured us. You have need of our mighty wings to carry you to the stars. We have recognized you,

Chicovaneg; your name tells us that you are des-
tined to light a new Sun. We will give you our
powerful wings."

Chicovaneg tied two of the great eagle wings
to his legs and two to his arms. And when the
eagles had taught him how to use them, he took
the two great birds under his arms and flew with
them to the rock Taquinvits. Here he put them in
a cavern where they would be sheltered from wild
animals, now that they were without their wings.

And the eagles said: "We will wait here until you kindle a new Sun. For in the new Sun, new wings will grow for us, and then we will fly to you, and greet you, Chicovaneg, for you are a friend of all that is good and noble on earth."

Chicovaneg said good-bye to the eagles and went to prepare himself for the final ascent from earth. When at last he was ready, he wore the powerful living eagle as a helmet. In his left hand he carried the marvelous shield made of the hides of great tigers and the skin of the mighty coatl tapir; in his right hand he carried a heavy spear with a long sparkling tip of gilded flint. He wore the mighty wings of the two eagles on his arms and legs. His body was clothed in hides of mountain lions, and over all he wore a cloak of feathers from the most brilliant and beautiful birds in the land of Chiilum. The soles of his feet were shod with leather sandals made from the skin of a young antelope. And thus, following the advice of the old sage in all its details, was he fitted with the strongest and swiftest things in this world.

Now he stood at the end of the world ready to begin his journey into the heavens. To the Feathered Serpent Chicovaneg said: "Let us start on our quest." And he looked up above him where rose the lowest star.

The Feathered Serpent answered: "Leap, Chicovaneg. I will guard you while you rise. Do not turn around, do not look back, but leap forward."

Chicovaneg crouched to spring into space. Then he saw that the lowest star was higher than he had judged it to be, and he was afraid, saying: "Feathered Serpent, what will happen if I jump too short and fall into the cold and endless void?"

Replied the Feathered Serpent: "Do not think of the cold and endless abyss. Leap for that little star you see there, right before your eyes."

Again Chicovaneg made ready to jump, and again he was afraid, saying: "The lowest star is much too high for me to reach. O Feathered Serpent, if only I stood upon a high rock. If it could

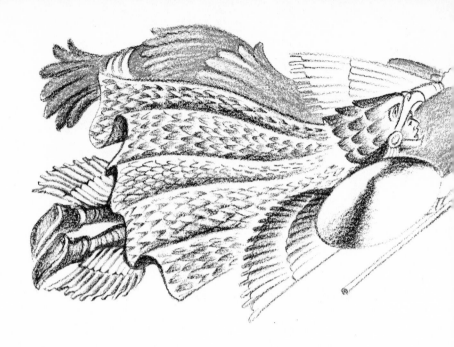

not be a high rock, then a mountain would do, or if it could not be a mountain, then I would be satisfied with a hill, and if it could not be a hill, I would be content with a palm tree. Yes, if I found a high palm tree, I would dare to leap to that little star yonder."

Again the Feathered Serpent advised: "Jump, Chicovaneg! Do not look down or back. Leap!"

Chicovaneg, still hesitating, now said: "My shield has loosened on my arm, so I must bind

it more tightly; and, see there, the thongs of my sandals are now slipping. These things must be fastened before I can leap, or I shall fail and fall into the bottomless abyss."

Patiently the Feathered Serpent watched him undo the straps and retie the thongs. And this took Chicovaneg many months. At last he was ready. Once more he crouched to spring, and once more he trembled as he looked at the lowest star.

"Jump, Chicovaneg. Do not look backward, or

down into the void." And when the Feathered Serpent saw that Chicovaneg still hesitated, it sprang and struck him in the back with such force that Chicovaneg flew forward like an arrow and fell headlong upon the lowest star, the Serpent behind him.

Now Chicovaneg rose proudly, looked for his great spear, cleaned the star dust from his garb of feathers and furs, and went to pay his respects to the Manes, the spirits of the deceased who guarded the star. They had black faces, for they were not of Indian blood.

When Chicovaneg told them how he had left his wife and son and all that he held dear on earth that he might create a new Sun for mankind, they made him welcome and freely gave him a piece of their star. Chicovaneg placed the star-fragment on his shield, where immediately it began to glow with great brilliance.

By the star glow on his shield, Chicovaneg could now see better in the dark void. From this moment on, he felt as sure and courageous as a young god. No longer did he hesitate in his course, but vaulted from star to star, the Serpent always with him. Though he appeared on each star uninvited and unexpected, the spirits made him welcome. And though from star to star their faces were black or yellow or white, and though the spirits were strange to him in their appearance and their speech, all of them gladly gave him bits of their star.

When Chicovaneg came at last to the spirits of his own tribe, he was welcomed with great festivities. The spirits of his own people were proud that one of their blood was to create the new Sun. They healed Chicovaneg's wounds and bade him rest while they repaired his weapons and his garb. His own forefathers recognized him and came forth to speak with him, to give him good counsel and wish him well.

Strengthened, and with new courage, Chicovaneg continued his difficult quest. And as he leaped from one star onward to another, his great shield glowed ever more brightly.

At last his shield became so brilliant that it was brighter than the biggest star. Then the evil gods saw with rage that Chicovaneg was well on his way to creating a new Sun, and they sought with great fury to destroy him. They caused the earth to shudder, and whenever Chicovaneg was about to leap to a star, they made the stars tremble. They knew that if he missed but once he would tumble into the cold dark void of the cosmos and fall forever, through all eternity. Not even the fabled magic of the sacred Feathered Serpent could save him then.

But Chicovaneg had become wise and patient in his wanderings. Obeying the suggestions given him by the spirits of his forefathers, he now did nothing with haste. He waited quietly until the great tremors of the earth and the stars subsided, and then—before they could begin again—he sprang across the perilous void. Sometimes when a star was beyond Chicovaneg's mightiest leap,

the Feathered Serpent flew ahead; his fangs seized
hold of the star's rim, and his tail swung down
into space. Then Chicovaneg leaped to catch the
brilliant tail and climbed up onto still another star.

· 33 ·

Chicovaneg climbed higher and higher, and his shield became brighter and brighter with every year, glowing so brilliantly that now men on earth could see that a new Sun was being kindled. How they rejoiced! In all their festivities they praised the coming of the new Sun in music and songs and dances.

The people on earth were able to see that Chicovaneg's journey had still to take him among dangerous comets. Each time he triumphed they were filled with joy. When it seemed that the distance from one star to another might be too great, they were filled with terror. And they went up to the highest mountains to build fires to signal to Chicovaneg their faith in him, their hope, and their desire to help light his way so he would not fail.

These distant earth fires gave Chicovaneg new strength and courage. For the forces of the evil gods battled him ceaselessly, hurling their spears and arrows and battle-axes and ever seeking to destroy him. But from star to star his shield glowed more brilliantly. And now when his enemies came too close, Chicovaneg held the shield before their faces and blinded them with its starry luster.

Protected by his bright shield, Chicovaneg loosed arrows and his spear with a sure hand. His spear he had fastened to a glistening lasso and the arrows to strong light tendons, so that he could always pull them back to him to use them again and again. And thus he was never without weapons, no matter on which star he stood.

Enraged by the courage and cleverness of Chicovaneg, the evil gods took revenge on the people of the earth. They sent over the lands sudden hurricanes which swept away huts and destroyed towns and ruined fields. They sent swarms of locusts, also hordes of rats over the earth and unloosed heavy floods. Out of mountains, fiery streams of molten rocks poured forth, and poisonous smoke filled the air. And so in this way did the powers of evil hope to destroy all life on earth before a new Sun would arise in the sky.

Then they hurled flaming rockets at Chicovaneg, so many indeed that to this very day, thousands of these fiery spears are still hurtling through the skies, now and then visible at night.

But in spite of all that and never seriously afraid of being hit by those fiery missiles, Chicovaneg climbed higher and higher, and his shield became brighter and brighter.

The earth responded to the new light.

Flowers began to grow and blossom anew.

Birds returned, with plumage more beautiful than before, and filled the air with song.

Trees shot up from the soil. Mangos and papayas and bananas began to ripen. Pears and tomatoes, mameys and zapotes and apples, cantaloupes and guayabas and anonas, coconuts and anacardos, watermelons, breadfruit, guanábanas, and chirimoyas began to appear on the earth.

Maize grew again, adorned with such long elotes and silken tresses and milky kernels that few people could recall its equal. Forests again were alive with all kinds of animals. Rivers and lakes swarmed with all kinds of fish.

One day the people looked up and became fully aware that high above them in the apex of the sky there was now truly a new Sun, perfect in its radiant glory. Then all people celebrated the great feast of the Sun in honor of Chicovaneg; and thousands came from far away to the places of the feasts. With great clamor and music, the festivities were opened in the city of Chamo. People came from Tila and from Shitalja and from Huistan. They came from Jovelto, from Oschuc, and from Bachajon, from Shcucchuits, Yajaton, and from Yalenchen. They came from Acayen and Nihich and from Natjolom and Huniquibal, from Sjoyyalo and Japalenque, Bilja, Jacotepec, Yealnabil, Sotsum, Tonaljá, Ishtacolcot, Chalchihuistan, Sibacja, and Chiilum—and from many other cities and villages and hamlets of the tribes and clans of all their nations.

And when the festival was at an end, the people went back to their homes to work with new

strength and happiness. They built new cities, beautiful temples, and high pyramids in honor of the Sun. They also built the holy city of Toniná, several leagues toward the sunrise of Hucutsin.

Even now the gods of darkness did not give up hope that they could blot out the light of the new Sun and rule mankind through terror and fear. They enveloped the earth with dark clouds so that men would forget Chicovaneg and worship the gods of evil. And under these heavy dark clouds, people began to fear and to despair and to suspect one another, for they now believed that the Sun would again be extinguished.

But Chicovaneg was on guard. He raised his great burning shield to protect the people on earth. And he cast burning spears from behind his flaming shield, striking at the evil ones who hid in the dark clouds. He pounded his shield so that the air under the sky trembled in dull thunder. And when again he had triumphed over the forces of evil, he was filled with joy, and he painted a great arc of beautiful colors in the sky, which was like an arching bridge from earth to sky on which the people's spirits might promenade if they wished to do so.

Chicovaneg's arc of colored air was his sign to all people on earth that they could work now in peace and happiness—he, the kindler of the new Sun, would stand guard. Never again would the Sun be extinguished.

Thus, says the old Mexican legend, did a brave young Indian man create a new Sun for mankind.

In the years that passed men realized that they enjoyed a beautiful Sun during the day, but they feared the darkness of the night. And so, according to the legend, the son of Chicovaneg set out on another journey to create for mankind a lesser Sun, one exclusively for the night.

And here is what the legend tells of that feature.

When the son of Chicovaneg grew up, the men of his tribe called him Huachinog-vaneg because he dreamed so much, and because his thoughts were more often in the sky with his father than on earth with his people. Often for long hours he sat in the shade of a tree, sad-faced and lost in meditation.

One day his mother Lequilants found him thus. "My son," she said, "why is it you are so sad? Everywhere people are happily rejoicing in the Sun your father gave them."

Huachinog-vaneg arose, bowed before his mother, put his face over her hand in greeting, and said, "Oh, my beloved and honored mother, and why should I not be sad? My father did great deeds on earth and in the skies. I feel unworthy of

my father and of you."

"My son," she told him, "you, too, are a creator. Do you not create beautiful houses out of stone, with sand and lime, so that people may live secure from storms and wild beasts?"

"It is true," the son replied, "but I have taught many to build as perfectly as I do. And time will decay these houses and also the temples and high pyramids I have built. After several summers no

person will remember the one who built them—
or even his name."

Whereupon the mother said, "My son, not all
men can create a new Sun, but there is ever a need
for houses to be built, for fields to be tilled, mats
to be woven, pots and plates to be made and
fired, and trees to be planted. For if all this were
not done, of what use would be the perfect Sun
in the sky?"

"Honored mother, you speak wisely. But you
are a woman, while I as a man, with different ways
and other thoughts, am driven on by ambition.
Many times when I have sat alone, under a tree,
I have spoken to my father. Know that it is my
ardent wish to go to him."

To this Lequilants said: "No mother, no wife
or lover has the strength to prevent a man of
strong mind from doing what he earnestly desires
to do. Take me to the house, my son. Let me lean
upon your arm, for now I feel my years."

The son saw his mother to the house. She put

out the light of the pine-wood torch and covered the embers on the hearth with ashes. But Huachi-nog-vaneg left the door open so that he might see the stars.

"Come here, my son," said his mother, "and sit beside me. I am afraid of the dark tonight as every night."

"Do not be afraid, mother. I am with you."

"Yes, my son, and I am glad. But there are mothers who have lost their sons, and mothers who are alone because their sons are far away, and there are those who never had a son. All are afraid of the dark night—as I am afraid when you are not here.

"I have thought at times that the people of earth also need a Sun at night. But who could create a Sun for the night only? It would be more difficult I think than it was to create the Sun for the day. The kindling of the Day Sun needed great courage, but only a man who is truly clever could create a Sun of the Night. For think! Such a Night Sun must give light but not heat; otherwise no living thing could recover from the day's heat, and all life on earth must sleep and rest and gain strength for the coming day."

Huachinog-vaneg pondered his mother's words. "You are wise, my mother," he said. "It would indeed be difficult to create such a Sun for the night."

"Imagine how difficult, my son!" said Lequilants. "For the Night Sun must not disturb mankind, neither the animals and plants of the earth in their rest. Nor should it shine always with a full light. Rather, its light should increase and decrease gradually so that earth's living things could grow accustomed to both light and darkness. And there should be nights on earth when the Night Sun disappears completely, so that people may know what true darkness means, and the usefulness of the stars and how satisfying complete stillness can be. How can any man on earth be clever enough to create such a Sun? Yet one dreams of such things as I often do."

Said Huachinog-vaneg, "It is a beautiful dream,

my mother, and I am happy you shared it with me."

Time passed. One day Lequilants found her son sitting on the ground, sketching many rings in the soil.

She came to him and said, "What thoughts are you lost in my son? A new building, or what?"

"I have thought much about your dream of a Sun for the night," he told her, "and now I believe I have discovered the way to create it. There is a very wise and learned man who all his life has studied the paths of celestial bodies. I am sure that with his guidance I can create the Night Sun which the world needs—one that you and all people on earth would like to enjoy, one that will give light but not heat, one that will slowly grow and then become small again, one that will even disappear at times so that its existence will be more appreciated by men."

Said Lequilants: "Go, my beloved son. My blessings are with you in all your wanderings and doings. Go and create a Sun of the Night so that mothers need not fear the darkness any longer. Should you meet your father, greet him for me and tell him that I think of him always in true love and admiration. When I look up in the dark sky and see that you have kindled the Sun of the Night, I shall know that my days are fulfilled, and that I can leave this earth as wife of the bravest man and mother of one of the cleverest men who ever lived."

Huachinog-vaneg went first to the sage Nahevaneg, and asked him, "O Wise Man, where can I find the Serpent with feathers? I need his help for I seek to create a Sun for the night."

Nahevaneg replied: "The Feathered Serpent is the symbol of our world, and as there can be only one such symbol, there is only one Feathered Serpent. Your father freed the Feathered Serpent to help him create the Sun. And after the Sun was kindled, he ordered the Feathered Serpent to stretch itself around the world where the arc of the sky rests on the earth or the great ocean. And there the Feathered Serpent lies to this day guarding the world against the evil forces that live beyond, always and forever ready to destroy the world.

"Your father is not only brave but also cunning. He knows that the Serpent likes to drink deeply of the sweet streams that flow along the horizon's edge, streams of morning dew from flowers that grow, some at sunrise, some at sunset, streams that mix with star dust to make a sweet and heavy wine of strange power. How the star dust sparkles in this rare wine! And how the Serpent loves it! This wine at the world's edge is the drink that alone can quench the Serpent's thirst. So Chicovaneg descends at the end of each day to see that the Feathered Serpent has not taken too much of this ethereal wine.

"When Chicovaneg finds the Serpent awake and on guard, his radiant face paints the evening sky a golden red. But when he finds the Serpent asleep or drowsy with wine, he is angry, and his eyes flash like fiery wings dipping in and out of the dark evening sky. So you see, Huachinogvaneg, the Serpent, busy as it is, cannot help you."

As the sage was speaking, a rabbit came jumping along, nibbling eagerly at the lush cool grass growing near their feet.

"Take a rabbit along with you, son," said the

sage. "A rabbit can leap, is a friendly companion, and can be of good use to you."

Huachinog-vaneg accepted the sage's counsel. He lifted the rabbit up by its ears and held it softly in his arms. Then he thanked Nahevaneg and bade him farewell.

Now Huachinog-vaneg set himself to the task of making two shields. As soon as he had found a convenient place to work he made a heavy shield to carry on his right arm. Then he made another of the fine silky fibers of the maguey plant. It was so light and wondrously woven that when he held

it against the Sun, he could see the Sun like a dark disk behind it. This shield he did not fasten to either arm, but carried it first in one hand, then in the other. He had no need of a spear, for he meant to follow the golden road his father had built from which all evil spirits had been driven back into darkness. In that bright light and always in full view of his father, he need fear no enemies.

He provided himself also with a strong and long lasso, and when finally he was ready, he took his rabbit—Tul by name—and traveled to the end of the world.

At the world's end there was a deep cavern in which lived the great tiger Cananpale-hetic. This tiger came out of his cavern and said to Huachinog-vaneg: "Do not fear me, for understand, I am the world tiger. Here is the very spot from which your father started on his journey. It was here he hesitated, because he feared to jump to the lowest star. Here in his hesitation he stamped one foot, and then the other, treading so hard that this cavern was formed. I fled here, pursued by savage coyotes which the evil gods sent to destroy me. It was then Chicovaneg saved me from the coyotes, and offered me this cavern as a home. And he sent the Feathered Serpent to kill the coyotes, so I was left in peace to heal my wounds. Now I remain here for eternity, to protect the road from the earth up to the lowest star.

"Rest here, Huachinog-vaneg, and gather strength for your difficult task. And your rabbit Tul may eat all it desires of the green prairie grass that lies around us."

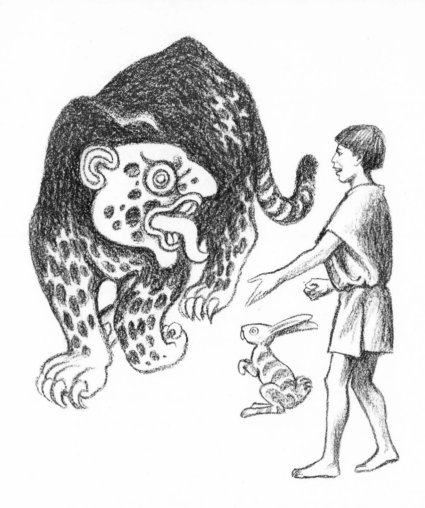

Huachinog-vaneg rested, and Tul ate well. Then together they climbed the rock Chabuquel.

Huachinog-vaneg looked at the lowest star and saw that it was too far away to reach in one leap. He became afraid and much discouraged, but Tul said, "I will go ahead and jump while you wait here. If I fall into the abyss of Balamilal, I alone will be lost. Find another rabbit then—there are many. I, myself, have a hundred and forty sons. You may select the strongest one, and tell him that I, his father, command him to follow you, and he will come."

Then Huachinog-vaneg said, "Hear me well, Tul. We are friends, and I do not want to lose you. Let us wait here until the rock Chabuquel has grown a little more; then the jump to the lowest star will be easier than it is today."

But the rabbit Tul replied, "My life is not so long as yours, Huachinog-vaneg. I cannot wait."

And before Huachinog-vaneg could reply, the rabbit Tul had jumped. He fell back at first without touching the lowest star. But he tried again and again, and at last the tip of one of his long ears touched the star, and he struggled with his legs to get a foothold. A branch of a thornbush helped Tul to scramble onto the star. Then free of the thorns, he leaped up onto a high rock, jumping up and down until Huachinog-vaneg could see him. Huachinog-vaneg threw his lasso to the star; Tul caught it and fastened it onto the peak of a rock, and Huachinog-vaneg swung through space on the lasso and landed on the star.

Together in triumph they went to greet the inhabitants of this first star.

And thus did they wander from star to star, taking only tiny fragments from each one; for the Sun of the Night did not need to be as large or as bright as the Sun of the Day. To make a lesser and cooler light than that of the great Sun, Huachinog-vaneg tied each bit of star as it was given him to his lasso and let it down into the black void to cool off.

And Huachinog-vaneg said to Tul: "My Sun will not be as beautiful or as marvelous as the Sun created by my father; but the Sun I have almost completed is as my mother wanted it, sometimes great, sometimes thin, and sometimes invisible."

"How clever you are!" said Tul. "How did you manage to do that?" And Huachinog-vaneg showed him. He took the shield in his left hand and moved it slowly in front of the shield of the Night Sun which was fastened on his right arm. As the shade of the lighter shield moved across the heavier shield, the Night Sun became smaller and smaller until it was completely shadowed and only its darkened outline was visible. And slowly, slowly, Huachinog-vaneg moved the lighter shield along, letting the Sun-of-the-Night shield become larger and larger until it regained its full size.

When his mother looked up at the sky and saw this, she called her neighbors together, and said: "Now I can lie down and die in peace, for I have done my duty on earth. I have repaid the good earth for the life it granted me. I had a brave husband, and I bore him a son who was wiser and cleverer than he." Saying this, she bent down to earth, and died on her knees.

The men of her tribe took her up to the highest mountain peak in the center of the land, where she would be closest to her husband and her son. And the sky covered her body with a white mantle

of eternal snow. The first ray that Chicovaneg sends to earth each morning kisses her forehead before it reaches other people, and the last ray in the evening envelops her body in a red-gold glory.

Huachinog-vaneg journeyed steadily across the firmament bringing the light of the Night Sun to mankind. And so faithfully did the Night Sun make its changes that people on earth came to look to it for the order of the days and the hours and the months and the tides.

Once Huachinog-vaneg stumbled on his way and was late in his journey, and the people became confused in their accounting of the time. And so it is to this day.

Wherever Huachinog-vaneg went, the rabbit Tul leaped in his way, full of pranks and play. Now Tul was in front, now behind, and now between his legs; at last Huachinog-vaneg became impatient with Tul's antics, and he said: "The people on earth will think that I stumble drunkenly across the heavens, and they will build no more temples to me and no pyramids, or any longer name days after me. It would be better for both of us if you went down to earth to join your family. You will live happily there, begetting perhaps a thousand more sons. I know that you love the nights more than the days, so when you wander at night longing to find the choicest cabbage leaves, I will send you the brightest light; my light will help you to see the coyotes or the wild cats who are after you. So I think it is time for you to go, Tul."

Tul knelt before Huachinog-vaneg and blinked, his eyes moist with tears, as he said: "I learned long ago that human beings do not know gratitude, Huachinog-vaneg. But you are not part of the people any more; you are a god now and people build temples and pyramids on earth in your honor. Now to my surprise I learn from you that even gods know no gratefulness. And I hoped that your people on earth would make me half a god, if not a whole one, for I helped you reach your first star, and I have been a true friend and useful companion to you since the day we met for the first time."

Huachinog-vaneg answered: "But don't you understand? You are in my way, leaping and jumping as you do. So leap and jump back to earth, Tul. I thank you for your help. Anyway, perhaps I might have found my way without you."

"I am not very sure of that," Tul replied. "For I remember too well how frightened you were, standing there by the cavern of the tiger, hopping from one foot to the other, afraid to make the leap. Now I'd have to jump from star to star to get back to earth from where we came, and my bones are old. If I fail in just one leap, I'll fall into the bottomless void, and go falling forever. You couldn't come to help me, now that your godly duty is to mark the times of the month and the year to people on earth.

"Or perhaps I would arrive on earth—but with broken legs, unable to search for my food at night or for the hole in which I lived with my family, no matter how much light you sent me. I'd be unable to escape from the coyotes and dogs trying to catch me. And should an eagle spy me, I wouldn't be able to sprint to a burrow before he'd swoop down and gobble me up. So, Huachinog-vaneg, like it or not, there's no other remedy, I'll leap around your legs as long as is good for my health."

Angered by these words, Huachinog-vaneg grabbed Tul by his long ears and lifted him to hurl him forevermore into the black void of Balamilal. But Tul turned his face to Huachinog-vaneg, grinned and blinked, and cheerfully kicked his legs above the black void to show he was not afraid. And seeing those great kicking legs Huachinog-vaneg suddenly remembered how this rabbit had leaped out into space for him, risking his life every time, over and over, so that he, Huachinog-vaneg, could become a god. And gratefulness rose up at last in his heart.

He embraced Tul and said to him: "You shall stay with me forever. I will put you in the middle of my great shield and carry you around with me

on my trips across the firmament. And the people down on earth shall see you there for ever and ever in the very center of my shield."

Then Huachinog-vaneg removed some of the little star-fragments from the middle of his big shield and set the rabbit Tul there, where he can be seen to this day.

And this is how the rabbit Tul became part of the Mexican people's calendar, as a grateful reminder of his help in kindling for them the glorious Sun of the Night.

B. Traven is the internationally known author of *The Treasure of the Sierra Madre, The Death Ship, The Bridge in the Jungle* and other novels. He personally directed the preparation of the first English edition of *The Creation of the Sun and the Moon*, his only children's book. Traven died in Mexico City in 1969.

Alberto Beltrán is one of Mexico's leading artists. A founder of the National Arts Academy in Mexico City, he has won several national and international prizes and has illustrated the work of such American writers as Victor W. Von Hagen and Oscar Lewis.